How to I

(When you

A simple guide to changin

By Jen Zead

First published in Great Britain 2021 by Klery Publishing.
Copyright © 2019 by Jen Zead

A copy of this title is available from the British Library. Paperback ISBN 978-1-8384178-0-2 Ebook ISBN 978-1-8384178-1-9

Typeset by Klery Publishing services.

Dedication:

This book is dedicated to
whomever thinks that climate change
is something that they can't influence.

And no, I will not be apologising for my poor attempts at
humour and pop culture references that are found within this
book. ☺

A little about me

Well, as you have probably read, my 'name' is Jen Zead. It's not my real name, although it would be super cool to have your last name as 'Zead'. I chose this as my pen name because it sounds like Gen Z, the generation that I'm in, and the generation who this book is intended for.

Well anyway, thank you for giving me your money so that I can buy that mansion on Rightmove…I'm joking! But jokes aside, by purchasing this book you should know that I will do my best to share a percentage of any profits to charities close to my heart … you see, you have already made a difference! Gold star for you!

Okay so 'a little bit about me'. I could say something like 'I have always had a keen interest in nature and the environment' but that's not necessarily true. Of course, I liked animals and… plants (?) as much as any seven-year-old would at that age, but I never really appreciated them as much as I have done for the past 3 or 4 years. I can't really pinpoint or remember even having that realisation of the existence of global warming. In fact, I think the first time I ever heard of global warming was in a Futurama episode that I watched when I was around eight. It didn't really strike me as something to be worried about, it was just a bunch of cartoon characters on TV.

The real 'journey' I guess started in 2017, when I became increasingly mindful of what I did, what I bought, what I consumed and the impact of all of this on our planet. I had tried to seek information to educate myself on what I could do to make things better. I remember having a 'light bulb' moment, sometime last year when I realised that no matter how many lights I switched off, or how many plastic bottles I didn't use, it still wouldn't change much. But then I thought … what if more people switched off lights or didn't use loads of plastic bottles? Every single one of those acts would soon add up! (Sorry, that this bit sounds like my villain origin story).

Right now, just think about how much energy we could save if hundreds of thousands of people switched off lights that weren't needed, out of habit, even though it still wouldn't change much, we would still be making a change. Think about that collective shift in buying trends when brands or corporations notice a change in the frequency of our buying habits and what items we're buying. They will have to change what they make available to us... they will do this to meet the market need, because at the end of the day, they just want to make money. (This definitely sounds like a villain origin story).

That collective change is something that we have in our control. You can't control everybody in the world, but you can control yourself. You can influence other people around you, like family and friends. If everybody who reads this book does just that, well, we could be on our way to fixing the planet (why do I sound like the old wise guy trope in movies?).

That's one of the things that prompted me to write this book and what motivated me to carry on writing. Well, that and the fact that nearly all 'eco-friendly advice' books were aimed towards adults.

And that's ~~how I met your mother~~ 'How to Fix the Planet (When You're a Teenager)' was born.

My 'book baby' is all grown up now and its ready to go into the world. Yes, it made me angry at times. Yes, some words were said and shouting involved. And sometimes it made me wish I had never thought to have a ~~child~~ book in the first place. But at the end of the day, it is my 'baby' and now I have to let it spread its wings (pages) and change the world. (I think I might get a dog as a replacement child to cope with my empty nest syndrome.)

FOREWORD

Climate change is THE greatest existential challenge to the future of humanity that has occurred since humans first walked the Earth some 2 million years ago. This is not to diminish the other catastrophes humanity has had to endure such as plagues and wars. Nor does this diminish potential future threats from rogue bio, nano or AI technologies, nor the remaining threats from asteroids or our massive stores of nuclear arms.

Rapid climate change has already begun. Hurricanes, tornadoes and wildfires are already growing in intensity and frequency as the temperatures begin to rise. Climate change threatens far more than the simple comforts of spending time outdoors - it will profoundly reshape economies and life around the globe. These dislocations will create daunting economic and physical challenges for people everywhere. Sadly, these impacts will also be unevenly felt. Many low-lying, coastal communities will be physically displaced. Some estimates now suggest that more than 500,000 people now live in low-lying areas that will become yearly flood plains. The fertility of farmland will be greatly impacted. All these effects are already happening, and it will get much worse.

It is now well understood that the main cause for this sudden and rapid onset of climate change is the direct result of the advancements of humanity as measured by population, the burning of fossil fuels, reduction in CO_2 capture due to deforestation and changes in land use. Even farming, ranching, and other forms of resource uses have an impact. Even IF humanity as a species managed to STOP emitting carbon immediately, it would still take decades for the Earth's climate to stabilize at a higher temperature (and the impacts of that to change).

Unfortunately, just putting on the brakes will no longer stop the vicious cycle we have already set in motion. One stark example is the melting of the polar ice caps. Until recently, the Northern Arctic had year-round ice which reflected sunlight and heat back into space. Over the last 10 years, the summer ice has melted away. Now, the summer ice is gone and the exposed dark seas absorb sunlight which is increasing the rate of global warming.

Ultimately, if we wish for human life on Earth to continue to thrive, human-caused climate change must be addressed now and by virtually everyone. Humanity will need to take massive steps to not only curb emissions, but extract greenhouse gases from the atmosphere, perhaps by creating artificial reflectivity in our skies, lands or oceans to reflect heat back into space.

But these steps are VERY hard. The technologies largely don't yet exist. And only a population already invested in solving these problems will take these steps. We need a global movement.

All great movements are founded by individuals and a few small groups, often of young activists. Successful movements focus on values and engagement over slogans and rhetoric. Clear minded, unwavering activists have always been the agents of change in our world. While governments of the world will have to work together to tackle the biggest items, they won't do their part until we, the people, are onboard doing our part, and demanding systemic change.

Jen Zead offers us an insightful, well researched, and inspirational guide to the important role each of us can, and indeed must take on, if we are to minimize the damage to our planet and our societies.

Whether you are already a climate convert in search of a good roadmap for how to help, or new to the understanding of the importance to take action, Jen Zead will guide us to help make better decisions. Better for ourselves, our communities and our world. I believe this book is a noteworthy piece of the complex puzzle we must solve. We all need to ask ourselves, "How to fix the planet (when you're a teenager)"

Richard Garriott de Cayeux

Explorer: The Poles, the Ocean Depths, 7 Continents, and the International Space Station

P.s. from Jen Zead – *I was ecstatic that Richard not only was happy to review my book but was delighted to provide the foreword! What a cool guy – thanks R* 👍

INTRODUCTION

I'm a believer that the biggest changes come from the smallest of acts. That the everyday decisions and actions we make can help to reduce our carbon emissions. 👍

As the adults of the next generation (scary, I know), we must take our future into our own hands. The Earth has looked after us for so many years, now it is our turn to look after the Earth, so that generations to come can continue to thrive in a sustainable way that works with our planet, not against it.

I've split this book into just five chapters, each covering a different issue and what you can do right now to make positive changes, based on my personal experience and research into these areas.

Even though this is a short book, I recommend that you don't read it in an afternoon after your lunch. I'd like you to spend time absorbing each chapter and reflect on it. This will help you to adapt to the changes more easily as well as helping the environment.

In all of the chapters, I discuss the issues at hand (fact checked by experts listed in the acknowledgements). At the end of each chapter, I provide suggestions (all tried and tested by me, so that they are easy at-home solutions) on what you can do to become more mindful of your lifestyle choices. And lucky you, I've also provided an 'End of Chapter Checklist' – so that you can look back at this as often as you like to check your progress and what else you can do (as you can see, I'm a sucker for a list and some good ol' written organisation).

This book isn't about me telling you that you must be vegan or live a zero-waste lifestyle, this is about how you can fix the planet. Wow, that last bit sounded dramatic (and corny) but seriously though, what better time to start than now? Let me show you a 'whole new world'... if you didn't get that reference I'll feel very embarrassed.

Food, the fact and the fiction

I feel that there is a lot of… let's just say, misleading information and a 'one size fits all' approach when it comes to food and climate change. Some news articles claim that 'everybody should be vegan in order to meet the 2030 climate target', while others state that 'eating meat has no links to the climate crisis'. In this chapter, I am going to be discussing the fact and fiction about food's relevance to climate change.

Just an F.Y.I, in case you didn't know, the 2030 climate target is the date set by the United Nations, where between now and then, if we reduce our carbon emissions by about 45%, we can limit the impact of climate change.

Link to the UN page on 'Transforming our world: the 2030 Agenda for Sustainable Development'

https://sdgs.un.org/2030agenda

Is there a relationship between food and climate change?

Yes, there is. Every piece of fruit, vegetable, meat, and any other food you can imagine, has a carbon footprint. A carbon footprint is the total amount of greenhouse gas emissions produced from something. This could be applied to people's behaviours or items of food. Some foods have a smaller carbon footprint than others. This is because a food's carbon footprint (or sometimes referred to as a foodprint…what a unique name!) is dependent on several factors, such as how it's grown, reared, farmed, processed, transported, stored, cooked, and disposed of. The lower the foodprint means that it is less harmful to the environment as less greenhouse gases are created in its production, which itself means less contribution to climate change.

(Wow, that last paragraph was wordy!)

Anyway, below is a table showing the foodprint for some foods.

Are you surprised by some of them?

Type of food	Carbon foodprint (measured in KG)
Beef	27
Cheese	13.5
Asparagus	8.9
Avocado	1.3

Sources: National Geographic (2016) and Business Insider (2015)

'Wow' count: 2

Is meat bad for the environment?

The high level of meat consumption is undeniably hurting the planet. This is because, like humans, livestock need vast amounts of food and water to grow properly. They also need land to be reared on. The amount of land required is relative to the animal itself (e.g. rearing cows would need more land than chickens because cows are larger animals). Animal agriculture is responsible for biodiversity loss, acid rain, water and land degradation, and deforestation. In summary, it's not looking good.

But it is important to keep in mind that these effects usually occur in countries where there are not enough (or any) laws that protect the environment from exhaustive livestock farming.

According to BBC News (2019), beef cattle raised on deforested land is responsible for 12 times more greenhouse gas emissions than cows reared on natural pastures, like in the UK.

Beef is a notable carbon-heavy meat. This is because cows are large animals that require lots of resources. They also excrete methane which is a greenhouse gas and is actually far worse than carbon dioxide …. this is definitely not looking good!

However, some meats have a lower foodprint than others. According to an article by the National Geographic (2019), switching beef with chicken, cuts your carbon footprint in half! This is because chickens are more efficient in converting feed into protein. This in turn, reduces the amount of land and energy used, resulting in a lower carbon footprint.

Is veganism the way to go?

In an ideal world where everybody has the same amount of money and everybody's body is exactly the same, the answer is yes.

A plant-based diet is undeniably better for the environment, but realistically speaking, the majority of people are unable to go completely vegan.

Everybody should definitely reduce their meat and dairy intake (if they can, but please consult with your doctor in case you have specific dietary needs), but whether you decide to take it to the next level is completely your choice.

Before going vegan, it is vital to do your research on nutritional information. I recommend you visit the Vegan Society website which provides a lot of information on what to eat when going vegan to avoid any deficiencies. This information was approved by the BDA (British Dietetic Association), so you know that you're in safe hands.☺

Can eating meat be eco-friendly?

Yes, it can, but moderation is key. To meet the 2030 climate target, we must reduce our meat intake by 70%. In an article by BBC Food, Chiara Vitali (Forests Campaigner, Greenpeace) says 'A 70% reduction looks like eating one portion of chicken and fish once a week and red meat once a month'.

If you really miss the taste of meat and can't bear the thought of having a portion of red meat once a month, try some meat alternatives! My family and I love 'Quorn * Mince' because it's versatile, and for a mid-week treat we have 'Linda McCartney's * Vegetarian Burger'.

In the U.S, companies such as Beyond Meat * and Impossible Foods * are doing really well at providing meat alternatives foods!

Fairtrade®

Fairtrade® is a scheme that ensures producers in developing countries receive a fair price and don't fall victim to slavery. Fairtrade * (as well as helping minorities with socioeconomic issues) sets environmental standards that all producers must comply with.

These standards include:

- ✔ Soil and water quality

- ✔ Biodiversity protection

- ✔ Pest management

- ✔ Energy and greenhouse gas emission reduction

- ✔ Waste management

- ✔ Prohibition of genetically modified organisms or harmful chemicals

Some farmers invest in environmental projects, such as the promotion of biodiversity or reforestation projects. Fairtrade ° products can easily be identified because of their well-known logo. As you can tell, I LOVE Fairtrade °, it supports and acts on values that are so important to me, we love to see it.

What are food miles?

These days, we can go to our local supermarket and buy a variety of fresh fruit and vegetables at any time of the year. This is because we have them imported from all around the world, right to our local supermarket. This leads me to the topic of this paragraph, which is food miles!

'Food miles' is the distance food is transported from producer to consumer. So that we can have, for example, traditionally summer fruits in the winter. This way of living isn't great for the environment. Transporting food over long distances produces large amounts of carbon dioxide.

Food miles doesn't just apply to fruit and vegetables, many other foods are imported overseas.

What can you do about food miles?

When buying food in the supermarket, it is always important to check the country of origin. It is always best (for the environment) to buy produce that is from your own country or a country in your continent, as it hasn't travelled a great distance. However, according to the NHS and UK government guidelines, it is recommended to eat 5 portions of a variety of fruits and vegetables every day. Following those guidelines and only buying produce that is seasonal can be difficult. Above all, stay healthy and if at times you are buying foods that were not produced in your country, don't beat yourself up about it. Please remember that you should always put your health over the environment. The message is to try to make some changes – just do your best! ☺

Moving back to labelling, if you live in the U.S, this information can be misleading. This is because foreign beef can legally be labelled as 'Product of the U.S.A' as long as it has been processed there.

If you're unsure where the meat was reared, encourage your family to buy from a local butcher. Butchers usually buy from local farms where farmers have to comply with environmental regulations (particularly soil and water conservation). Bear in mind that environmental regulations for livestock farming differ in each country.

A simple solution to reduce your food miles is to take a packed lunch into school or work instead of getting it from the canteen. Not only will it be better for the environment (because there are no added food miles from transport), but you can make anything for your lunch that you know you will enjoy and it is also much more cost-efficient!

Getting your family involved

Okay, you may be thinking 'Great! I now know how to reduce my foodprint, but how do I convince my family to reduce theirs?'.

Here are a few ideas of what you can do to help your family eat more environmentally friendly.

Get more involved in the meal planning:

You can't expect your family to do all of the research into environmentally-friendly meals - you have to make some sort of effort by planning meals and helping to write the shopping list. This will show your family that you're taking initiative, and they will be more willing to reduce their meat intake, eat more fruit and vegetables, etcetera.

Explain why it is better for the environment:

You need to show your family how important this is to you. Mention some of the things I have discussed in this chapter.

Do some cooking yourself:

I understand that we as students are incredibly busy with studying and homework, so cooking for the family isn't always possible. However, if you cook just every other Saturday (or any other day of the week), it will make a difference. First of all, you will be in complete control of what your family is eating, and second of all, I'm sure the person in your family who usually cooks will love someone else cooking for them!

What you can do this week

- Can you remember what meals you had this week? If you can, write them down.
- How much meat did you have in that week?
- Go to your fridge and look at the labels on the food items. How many of them were produced overseas?
- Talk to your parents/guardians about eating more environmentally-friendly. Tell them why it's important to you and what you're going to do.
- Help with the meal planning and shopping list for that week.
- Go shopping with one of your family members/guardians. Maybe visit a local farmers market.
- Take a packed lunch to school.
- Substitute one meat meal with a vegan or vegetarian one (if you can).
- Reduce your food miles. Replace one to three fruit or vegetable items with seasonal alternatives, if possible.
- Cook a vegan or vegetarian meal.

Well done for completing this week's chapter!

End of chapter checklist ✔

1. Eat one portion of chicken and one portion of fish a week (if possible).

2. Limit your red meat consumption to once a month (if possible).

3. Continue to help with meal planning and shopping.
   Eat more fruit and vegetables (try to make sure that some are seasonal).

4. Take a packed lunch to school.

5. Make takeaways a treat to reduce food miles.

6. Buy local produce (if possible).

7. Purchase Fairtrade® products (if possible).

Plastic, the big debate

Plastic first became popular in the 1960s. It was cheap, durable and convenient for the average citizen, and now it is polluting our oceans and countries. Wow, that last sentence sounded depressing, but it's unfortunately our reality.

'Wow' count: 3

Plastic waste is increasing at an alarming rate. By 2050 it is predicted that there will be more plastic in the ocean than fish (scary fact)! The WWF calculated that the UK generated a staggering amount of 4.9 million tonnes of plastic waste in 2014 alone (another scary fact). So, how do we tackle this huge issue and get rid of the scary facts?

In this chapter, I'm aiming to inform you (wow that sounds formal) about plastic pollution and give you guidance to help you reduce your plastic waste in a realistic way.

'Wow' count: 4

Climate change and plastic

Most plastics are derived from fossil fuels (*shakes head*). The process of acquiring and transporting those fossil fuels for plastic production and disposal creates billions of tonnes of greenhouse gases (that's a lot) which contributes to climate change (*shakes head again*). However, the nightmare doesn't end there. If the plastic isn't recycled, it ends up in landfills, or worse still, gets dumped in the sea. When the plastic ends up in the ocean, the sunlight could cause the plastic to release even more greenhouse gases (if it floats). Most plastics sink and damage sea creatures and the ecosystems ☹.

What is virgin plastic?

Virgin plastic is plastic that has been made newly, without any recycled materials. When you can, purchase products that are not made from virgin plastic. Buy products that are made from recycled materials. Look for the sign rPET on your drink bottles – this means that the PET used to make this bottle is recycled. Or you could just avoid buying plastic items in the first place. Look for bamboo, or glass alternatives (anything that you know can be easily recycled). There are some amazing new items and packaging out there.

What are microplastics?

Microplastics are small pieces of plastic less than 0.2 inches (5mm) in diameter. Most microplastics are produced by a plastic product that breaks down during use. Once produced, they make their way into everything: rivers, oceans, fish, soils and even the air. Microplastics are produced by some suntan lotions, wet wipes, most clothing (see later chapters) etc.

This issue is bigger than recycling, so we need government bans on the sale of products that have the potential to leave behind microplastics.

What is zero waste?

I'm sure that if you've researched into reducing your plastic waste, you have stumbled across the term 'zero waste'. Lots of people define zero waste differently, but the most common definition (well, social media's definition, but I'll get more into that next) is 'eliminating your waste completely'.

The issues with the zero waste movement

One issue about this movement is the negative stigma around plastic. Let me just clarify that plastic itself is not the problem, but rather the unnecessary and unregulated use. I agree that there are certain items which do not need to be packaged in plastic but I have to disagree with zero wasters when it comes to things such as personal hygiene and health.

For example, plastic syringes are disposable to reduce disease transmission. Pill capsules that are made of plastic make sure that the correct dosage is released gradually. Some non-hormonal contraception methods are made of plastic and have many benefits, such as reducing the risk of reproductive cancers, pregnancy-related mortality, STDs, and not to mention the prevention of pregnancy. And those are just a handful of examples that demonstrate the benefits of plastic in the healthcare industry.

Another issue with the zero waste movement is classism. Classism is prejudice against people belonging to a particular social class. Zero waste products are not affordable or easily accessible for the majority of people. Zero waste products are clearly marketed at wealthier groups of people, but this is not right. Zero waste products should be made more affordable for all in order to make a large impact. In this way, everyone has the chance to reduce the amount of plastic they use.

The problem with this movement isn't the actual idea, but social media's interpretation of it - bear with me for this one.

I went to good old Wikipedia for a definition, and I couldn't have put this in better words myself.

'Zero waste is more of a **goal or ideal** rather than a **hard target**. Zero waste provides **guiding principles** for continually working towards eliminating waste.'

Remember that when considering zero waste, it is an **ideal**. Zero waste refers to system changes, so that this current waste problem we have isn't a problem in the first place.

It shouldn't be interpreted as a lifestyle change like veganism because it's practically impossible to live zero waste when there are currently only extremely limited or expensive options. The majority of us aren't able to live a completely zero waste lifestyle at the moment, but until the manufacturers and packaging people catch up, what you can do is try to purchase zero waste products when you can. Don't feel disheartened if you aren't able to do this all the time. Remember: you didn't create the plastic.

The main message I want you to take away from this is that nobody can be completely zero waste (due to accessibility, finance, health, and hygiene reasons), and that's fine! To quote Anne Marie Bonneau, 'We don't need a handful of people doing zero waste perfectly. We need millions of people doing it imperfectly.' I couldn't agree more.

The sure way to reduce your waste is to just buy less (when possible). It's just as simple as that. Buy even just 80% of what you already do, and you've cut down your waste by 20%! Wow!

'Wow' count: 5...?

Sorry if I sounded a tad intense before but I just needed to get that out of my mind for my own sanity!

Recycling: what actually happens to our waste?

For years, we've been told that recycling is the solution to plastic pollution (poet of the year right here...Ha!), and then we see the heart-wrenching videos of marine animals tangled in plastic. Plastic we thought was being recycled. So, what actually happens to our waste?

A little over a year ago, I watched the BBC documentary 'War on Plastic'. Anita Rani and Hugh Fearnley-Whittingstall embarked on the journey to discover where the plastic problem was coming from and what we can do to solve this. Watching this documentary, I saw that the UK was sending out tonnes of plastic waste to countries like Malaysia and leaving the locals to deal with it and suffer.

Shock and disgust were the emotions I felt upon seeing this. I also felt that I had been deceived, as I wasn't aware that my plastic waste was being sent overseas. The UK, however, isn't the only culprit. The US, Canada and Australia unfortunately all do the same. (Noticing a theme here....)

Following this documentary, I embarked on my zero waste quest. Spoiler alert: it didn't go well! I found some problems on the way, aside from the finance factor (the main drawback for a teenage girl who doesn't earn an income). After quitting the zero waste journey, I began to look for ways I could help the environment in a more realistic and sustainable way. I also wanted to understand why our plastic waste was being sent to other countries.

Why does our waste get sent to other countries?

It's simply because it's cheaper to export it overseas to be recycled.

Contaminated waste

Contaminated waste is when non-recyclable material ends up in the recycling stream. This means that the non-recyclable material travels through the recycling system whilst damaging perfectly fine recyclable materials. Also, the mixture is too difficult to separate and so none of it ends up being recycled.

Contaminated waste can also refer to when containers have not been cleaned properly, more specifically food containers. This is an issue as it may attract pests or cause blockages in machines.

This makes it uneconomic to recycle.

China has actually been sent illegal amounts of contaminated waste by waste management companies in the past, simply because the companies don't want to deal with it.

The root of the issue of contaminated waste is due to the fact that lots of people are unsure what can and can't be recycled. This is due to the lack of accessible information provided by governments (in some countries).

YouGov found that nearly 50% of the UK public find that information on recycling is unclear. I've done a bit of digging to help you.

So, what can be recycled?

Which types of plastic can be recycled?

Technically, all types of plastic are recyclable, but some are more difficult to recycle than others. Thermoplastics (e.g. plastic bottles) melt when heated so they can be reshaped and reused effortlessly.

However, thermosetting plastics (e.g., laptop chargers, which have been created in a way to withstand heat) burn when heated and release high amounts of carbon dioxide and toxic gas which is bad for both the environment and the health of people who are nearby.

Every country has different rules for recycling. These rules can sometimes be universal within a country, but most countries have different rules for recycling in each constituency. In the UK, each local authority has their own rules on what can and can't be recycled. To find out what your area accepts, search 'Recycling Locator' (https://www.recyclenow.com/local-recycling).

Go onto the website and click on 'What to put in your recycling at home', then enter your postcode and click on the different bins to find out what can be recycled. (This information is only relevant to UK residents).

I'm unsure on the specific rules for recycling in other countries, but you can usually find information on how to recycle on the official website of your government's environmental agency.

TerraCycle®

There might be some plastic items that you feel you can't live without, and they can't be recycled by your constituency. Don't worry! Use TerraCycle instead. https://www.terracycle.com/en-GB/

TerraCycle is a recycling company that has multiple drop-off locations in 20 different countries around the world to recycle the 'unrecyclable'. They have many free recycling programmes for different waste streams (that you can browse on their website), and you can find the closest drop-off location to you on their map.

The countries they operate in include:
Australia
Austria
Belgium
Brazil
Canada
China
Denmark
France
Germany
Ireland
Japan
Mexico
Netherlands
New Zealand
Norway
Spain
South Korea
Sweden
Switzerland
U.K
U.S.A

And yes, I put this list into alphabetical order by choice.☺

How TerraCycle ® works and why they can recycle items of waste that councils and local authorities can't

While almost all waste is technically recyclable, it's often too expensive for councils to recycle more complex materials which is why you can't put them in your green recycling bin at home.

Items such as crisp packets for example are made from a complicated mix of materials which require specific machinery and techniques to recycle. This makes the recycling process itself very expensive when compared to the value of the end product, and so the economics simply do not work.

To solve this issue, TerraCycle ® partners with brand sponsors to offer free nationwide recycling programmes to the public.

These brand partners cover the costs of transporting and processing the waste, as well as a charitable reward to members of the public who sign up to the programmes and send their waste into TerraCycle ®.

In the UK, TerraCycle® work with brands like McVitie's ®and Jacob's ® who sponsor biscuit and snack wrappers, allowing members of the public to sign up on the TerraCycle ® website and set up a drop-off location on behalf of their whole community!

However, TerraCycle® doesn't recycle crisp packets into other crisp packets. They are converted into composite plastic products like park benches. That sounds ok, but we buy billions of crisps a year and we don't need that many park benches!

There's nothing wrong with TerraCycle ®, but it is just an interim solution.

Why recycling is not the answer...yet

At the moment, the current recycling system is not as effective as it could be. This is due to a number of factors that are in no way a fault on the consumers behalf. *Looks at governments and big corporations*.

One factor includes the continued production of virgin plastics. Virgin plastics, as I mentioned before, not only release huge amounts of greenhouse gases in production, but they are the main reason why recycling is not yet... well, working. This is because the production of virgin plastics results in more plastics being introduced into the recycling chain, causing more plastics having to be 'recycled'. This subsequently causes more plastic to be burnt, dumped, or anything apart from recycled. Basically, the circle will just continue to expand until we are unable to cope with the mountains of plastics.

Ideally, governments should put a tax on the production of virgin plastics (with obvious exceptions) until the recycling technology becomes more advanced, so that corporations have no choice but to use recycled plastic. However, we do not yet live in an ideal world, so the best current option is to avoid buying items packaged or made from virgin plastics if possible.

The type of plastic is also vital in order for recycling to work. Most plastic can be recycled 5-10 times before its quality starts to degrade. To tackle this issue, there should be a wider use of chemical recycling. Chemical recycling is a process where the plastic can be broken down into its molecular parts. These are then used to make more plastic. Scientists at the U.S. Department of Energy's Lawrence Berkeley National Laboratory in Northern California have developed PDK plastic, a plastic that can be chemically recycled easily. This can help to close the plastic waste stream, when all plastics can be chemically recycled.

Governments should also make information on recycling clearer, because recycling can work, just not now.

We need to move to a system where every piece of plastic packaging is fully recyclable back into packaging or compostable. This is the aim of the UK Plastic Pact by 2025 to make this happen. Many brands including the likes of Unilever® and Tesco® have signed up.

The science bit! Ethylene is the main component used to make virgin plastics. This is a by-product of the whole crude oil breakdown process which gives us diesel. The problem would be that if we didn't use the Ethylene by-product, they would need to burn it off which would cause high levels of carbon dioxide being pumped into the atmosphere. Maybe the answer is that the whole cycle needs to be reduced. That is to say, if we reduce the crude oil needed, we reduce the amount the virgin plastic we create. So maybe it's not that hard after all? *Dusts off hands thinking that I've just single handedly solved the plastic crisis*

Biodegradable products - too good to be true?

Biodegradable products look the same as their plastic equivalent and claim to degrade faster. Most people will just put these products into the general waste bin after using them, not thinking about it twice because it's 'biodegradable'.

However, these products disrupt the waste stream as the recycling operatives aren't going to know if that make-up wipe is biodegradable or not, so it's eventually going to be sent to a landfill or the ocean (or be burnt).

A lot of plastics labelled biodegradable, like shopping bags, will only be eaten by microorganisms under very specific conditions of industrial composting such as a temperature of 60°C, and that is not the ocean. They are also not buoyant, so they're going to sink, meaning they won't be exposed to UV and break down.

It is also likely that marine animals will mistake them as food or become entangled in them, causing them a number of avoidable issues.

Biodegradable plastics are only eco-friendly if they end up being industrially composted to create compost which is used to grow crops.

Also, why not change some of your plastic stuff for non-plastic alternatives – reusable is best where you can.

What you can do this week

Go around your house and look in cupboards. Count how many plastic items or packaging you can see, don't do this if you know that it's going to stress you out.

- Go online to find out what your constituency can and can't recycle.

- Go onto TerraCycle® to find out what they can recycle.

- Think of swaps you can make for some items that can't be recycled.

- Look at brands that package their products in recycled materials.

- Create a better recycling system in your home. Have a bin for plastic for your council and a bin for plastic for TerraCycle®. You can even put images on your bin to show what can be recycled.

- When shopping, bring your own reusable bag because the production of paper bags releases 4 times more carbon emissions than a plastic bag.

- Purchase some plastic-free things if you don't already have them, e.g. a reusable water bottle.

- Give yourself a challenge if you can! Go to your bathroom and choose a certain number plastic items that you want to keep. Find plastic alternatives for all the other plastic items!

- Talk to family members about plastic pollution and what they can do to help.

Well done for completing this week's chapter!

End of chapter checklist ✔

1. Do some swaps for plastic items if possible.

2. Try finding multiple uses for one item or share a product with a family member when possible.

3. Check what can be recycled by your constituency.

4. Clean plastic packaging before sending it to be recycled.

5. Use Terracycle for things that can't be recycled by your constituency.

6. Be careful about biodegradable products.

7. Avoid buying products made from or packaged in virgin plastic.

8. Reduce the amount of plastic you buy in the first place.

9. Avoid buying products that cannot be recycled by TerraCycle® or your constituency.

10. Find uses for plastic packaging after you've used them (do some fun DIYs or just keep it because you never know when you might need it but don't become a hoarder).

11. Inform people you know about plastic pollution and what they can do to minimise their plastic waste.

Reminder: the most eco-friendly thing that you can do, is to use the stuff that you already have!

What's the problem
with Palm Oil

When I started becoming more 'environmentally aware', I didn't know a lot about Palm Oil. I actually first heard about it in a school assembly, I heard that it was terrible for the environment and it was pretty much in most foods and products. I felt so guilty about everything I was using. When I started writing this book, I knew that I must write a chapter about Palm Oil, and I discovered the truth *dramatic as it sounds* about this seemingly 'evil' vegetable oil. In this chapter I'm going to share the facts and try to figure out, what's the problem with Palm Oil. See what I did there, …the chapter title, …oh never mind.

What is palm oil?

Palm oil is an edible vegetable oil derived from the fruit of oil palm trees. According to WWF, it is found in up to 50% of packaged products in the average supermarket.

How does it affect the environment?

Palm oil production is one of the main causes of deforestation, and this leads to a number of environmental issues.

Rainforests support 46% of all living terrestrial carbon and 11% of the world's soil carbon. This means that when the trees are cut (especially the big old ones), this suddenly causes large amounts of carbon to be released into the atmosphere.

The deforestation aspect of sourcing palm oil directly impacts and threatens a number of species and biodiversity.

The only time when soil carbon is really important is when people clear peat forest to grow crops - this is because peat stores huge amounts of carbon (because the water stops plant matter being broken down). In this case, it isn't the deforestation that is causing the soil carbon emissions.

Oil palm can't grow in water-logged soils, so the peat is drained. Once the water is gone, the dead plant matter breaks down fast, releasing carbon that has been stored for thousands of years into the atmosphere. It also catches fire easily which is why there are huge problems with haze in South East Asia in dry years. Fires release carbon but also other air pollutants which cause problems for human and wildlife health.

Is palm oil the problem?

Palm oil is not necessarily the problem, it's just the irresponsible and unregulated sourcing that is causing these negative environmental impacts. Palm oil is very effective in the terms that it yields the most amount of oil, compared to other vegetable oil crops. In fact, according to the WWF, 'to get the same amount of alternative oils like soybean or coconut oil, you would need anything between 4 and 10 times more land'. This would create even bigger environmental problems than the ones we already face. Palm oil is also an important crop for many farmers in developing nations, so boycotting palm oil would affect the farmers and their families significantly.

What should you do?

In 2012, the UK government made a commitment for 100% of the palm oil used in the UK to be sustainable. In 2016, 75% of the palm oil was sustainable, and progress is still being made, but it takes an effort on the consumer's behalf as well to make a positive impact.

Whenever purchasing a product, you should always check if the parent company of the product is a member of the RSPO. The

RSPO (Roundtable on Sustainable Palm Oil) https://www.rspo.org/ is a third-party standard that helps companies to achieve their commitments on sustainable palm oil that benefits both the people and the planet. RSPO members are also not allowed to plant new plantations on peat, and in old plantations they have to manage the amount of water that they use to minimise the amount of carbon loss.

Another thing you should do is use the WWF scorecard http://palmoilscorecard.panda.org/. The WWF scorecard assesses retailer's, manufacturer's and food service's commitments and actions towards more sustainable palm oil. They're given a score out of 22, and this score is determined by a number of different factors. A high score means that they are very good at using sustainable palm oil.

Other names for palm oil

Some companies are quite sneaky and try to use other names for palm oil in the ingredient list of a product. *Puts on environmental detective hat* Any ingredient that has 'palm', 'stear', 'laur', or 'glyc' in it is probably a derivative of palm oil.

What you can do this week

- Look at some items you have in your house. Can you see palm oil in the ingredient list? Is that item from a company that is a member of the RSPO?

- Look at some companies on the WWF scoreboard. How do they rank?

- Talk to your family and friends about irresponsible palm oil farming.

Well done for completing this week's chapter!

End of chapter checklist ✔

1. Avoid buying products that contain palm oil from companies that are not in the RSPO.

2. Purchase products from companies that are members of the RSPO.

3. Check the WWF scorecard to see which companies have the highest and lowest score.

4. Inform other people about sustainable palm oil.

5. Inform other people that palm oil is not the problem itself.

The damage your wardrobe does

What better way to start an important chapter with a classic 'did you know' question! Okay, I'll start, *ahem* did you know that 10,000 litres of water are needed to make a single pair of jeans?

That's right, you guessed it (or read the chapter title)! We're going to talking about...*drum roll*...clothes!

In this chapter, I'm aiming to inform you how much damage your wardrobe does and what you can do to help reduce your impact!: United Nations 2019

What is fast fashion?

Ever go into a shop one week, and the next week that t-shirt isn't there anymore? That's fast fashion. Fast fashion is the rapid production of clothes to adjust to the latest trends whilst putting them on the market at a cheap price. They're also made from low quality materials by underpaid workers in order for companies to keep their production cost low but their profit high. These clothes will usually only be intact for a few wears, so the consumer will go back to the shop to buy new clothes and the cycle will just keep going on, and on, and on.

Social impacts of fast fashion

Companies tend to employ workers in poorer countries and take advantage of them (*shakes head at capitalism*) to receive a big profit. They give them an unacceptably low salary for 14-16 hour shifts, 7 days a week, in extremely poor working conditions. Some companies use the excuse 'it's better that we employ them than they don't have any work' and to a very small extent, that is true, but the majority of these manufacturing countries have a minimum wage which is a fifth of the country's living wage. The living wage is supposed to accommodate the basics such as food, rent, etc. This means that the workers are being paid less than what is needed to live.

Also, garment workers are exposed to hazardous conditions. In 2013, the Rana Plaza tragically collapsed and killed at least 1,100 workers. And this unfortunately only scratches the surface of the inhumane conditions that the majority of garment workers have to face on a daily basis.

Furthermore, 80% of garment workers are women and they're victim to sexual harassment and assault. Also, most companies won't allow them to go on maternity leave, putting the mother and unborn child at risk of a number of preventable health conditions. In some cases, pregnant women are forced to resign. This can cause stress and depression for the mother which can impact the child.

https://www.theguardian.com/sustainable-business/2016/mar/08/fashion-industry-protect-women-unsafe-low-wages-harassment

Don't worry if you're feeling sad and confused. The rest of this chapter is especially dedicated for what you can do to help.

How to recognise fast fashion

There are a few signs to look out for when trying to recognise a fast fashion brand.

- Low price - by low, I mean ridiculously low, like a pair of jeans that costs £10.

- Do the clothes closely match the latest trends?

- Look at news articles about that brand (this has really helped me in deciding which brands I want avoid).

Environmental impacts of fast fashion

The fashion industry is a notoriously large polluter. Some of the troubling issues that it causes includes soil degradation, water pollution, ocean pollution, greenhouse gas emissions, deforestation, waste, and more.

There are many statistics out there, but these are from the link below from Greenpeace.

- In the last 15 years, we have doubled how much clothing we make.

- People are more inclined now to throw away garments. Since 2000, this has increased by 36%. That is the equivalent of £140 million worth of clothing sent to landfill.

Materials

Materials give us an understanding of the environmental effects of that item of clothing. This helps us as consumers to make more mindful decisions of what we choose to buy and wear. Below are some of the most common materials and their environmental cost.

Cotton- cotton needs huge amounts of water and is usually produced in dry climates. This has had a huge impact on places such as the Aral Sea, where the production of cotton has led the area to be drained of water. It can take 2,700 litres to produce the cotton needed to make a single t-shirt.

https://www.worldwildlife.org/stories/the-impact-of-a-cotton-t-shirt

Cashmere- the overgrazing of sheep and goats, who are being used for their wool, has led to soil degradation. We need healthy soil for food production and to absorb carbon dioxide from the atmosphere. One area being impacted greatly by this is Mongolia where around 70% of all grazing land has been degraded. In the article below, you can read more about this.

Synthetic materials such as polyester and polyamide when washed, release microfibres. These microfibres make their way into the ocean and are consumed by aquatic organisms. These organisms are eaten by fish and eventually they make their way into our food chain (karma).

This is another form of microplastics, which we discussed in previous chapters.

Synthetic materials are made from fossil fuels which will then cause large amounts of carbon to be emitted into the atmosphere.

Rayon, modal and viscose- each year, thousands of trees are cut down and replaced with others to produce materials such as rayon, modal and viscose. The deforestation is not only detrimental to the environment, but it also threatens indigenous communities. There is also the issue that land should be prioritized for food crops.

Materials that are environmentally-friendly:

The wonderful site 'Sustain your Style' https://www.sustainyourstyle. org/en/fiber-ecoreview composed a table of environmentally-friendly fibres which I have put into a list below:

- Recycled polyester

- Organic cotton

- Alpaca fur

- Lyocell/Tencell *

- Recycled nylon

- Linen

- Silk

- Orange fibre

- Recycled cotton

- Hemp

- Responsible wool

- Pineapple fibre

- Recycled wool

- Ramie

- Responsible cashmere

- Refibra™

- Responsible leather

- Sustainable bamboo

I'm not saying that you're only allowed to buy clothes made from these materials, this list is purely for educational/advice purposes.

Hot off the press!

This is seriously 'news just in'! The amazing Bruna told me only today of some amazing new material routes. What this means is that there are a number of new companies and technologies out there that have started up, looking to make materials for clothing more sustainable. Through new efficient farming techniques and or new technologies. As an example, a company called Materna is spearheading these approaches to help the fashion industry be more net-positive. Materna are focusing currently on cotton but do look out for such companies via social media and do support them where you can. Check out the Materna site for more information https://www.materra.tech

Country of origin

Different countries have different laws for labelling the country of origin on clothes. For example, in the UK it is essential to state the country that manufactured the clothes. Whereas in EU countries, the rules for labelling the country of origin is not universal among its members.

Usually, clothes will be labelled with the country of manufacture.

It is important to know the country of origin because this gives us an insight into what the environmental standards are like, what the workers' rights are like, whether the country mainly uses renewable energy, etcetera.

Where to buy clothes

When buying new clothes first ask yourself, do you really need it? By this I mean, are you just buying it because you want it and it's trendy? Obviously, you are allowed to purchase something that you want, but I don't recommend buying things without mulling it over so that you don't regret it later (trust me, I'm all too familiar with that feeling).

To help you differentiate between what you actually like and trends (because it's difficult, especially when bucket hats are all over your Instagram feed), I recommend that you find your style! Your style doesn't have to fit a particular box. Experiment with different styles and see what feels good for you!

To do this mindfully, first go through your wardrobe to see which clothes you like and others which…you don't like too much but don't get rid of all your clothes just yet! Put them to one side for now. Next go through your siblings or parents etc wardrobe … with their permission (of course) and see if there is anything in there that you like the look of. I personally have raided both of my parents wardrobes and have dug out some decent clothes.

Nothing that you like? You could create a Pinterest board, a physical mood board (in a scrap book), or just save pictures on the internet or Instagram that you like. Then have a look through your clothes or mood boards and think to yourself that maybe you like a particular colour palette, or silhouette, et cetera you'll get the idea.

I'm no fashion/style expert, but there are loads of videos and articles on the internet and YouTube that can help you ☺.

I side-tracked a bit but I'm back now! Okay so, lots of people suggest that one of the ways to reduce your fashion footprint is to shop at ethical stores.

However, most ethical stores sell clothes that are a bit too pricey for the majority of people because they're meant to be investment pieces. But there are other ways to reduce your impact without going broke. However, if you can afford to shop at ethical stores, I really do encourage you to do so. My favourite ethical clothing stores that aren't overly expensive but are on the pricier side include 'Lucy and Yak', and 'nu-in'.

One place to buy affordable clothes is from a thrift/charity shop. Although this may seem unappealing to you, there's no harm in browsing. Who knows, you might actually snag a really good piece of clothing. You can even alter the item to however you would like it to look!

An alternative to thrifting is buying second hand from apps like DEPOP https://www.depop.com/. You can pretty much find anything you want on DEPOP and you're purchasing a pre-loved piece - it's a win-win! You can even sell clothes that you don't want any more on DEPOP! Another service similar to DEPOP is ThredUp (https://www.thredup.com/), they have many second-hand items from popular brands such as H&M and Hollister. There are loads of other second-hand clothing sites and apps out there as well. I was recently alerted to Vestiaire Collective https://www.vestiairecollective.com. This site is great for buying, selling and sharing pre-owned high-end clothes, if that's more your thing.

However, if you are in the unfortunate situation where charity shops are unavailable or you can't use apps like DEPOP, then the only option is to purchase fast fashion. But some fast fashion brands are more environmentally friendly than others.

Download the 'Good On You' (https://goodonyou.eco/) app or use their website. They assess brands out of five on their environmental and social impact and their treatment to animals. There, you can see which fast fashion brands are better than others.

When you are buying from fast fashion, try to reduce the amount and frequency of items that you buy. This will mean that you'll wear it more often because you don't have hundreds of clothes. I've heard that you have to wear a piece of clothing a minimum of 30 times for it to equal its environmental impact!

But above all, the most eco-friendly thing that you can do, is to use the clothes you already have! If you don't like a particular item, alter it, paint it, tie-dye it! Do whatever you want!

Rent-your-clothes

There are Apps that can help you access rentals of great clothes. You can rent your own clothes as a bit of a side-hustle or rent someone else's clothes!

- https://www.hurrcollective.com

- https://onloan.co

- https://hire.girlmeetsdress.com

- https://www.byrotation.com

- https://www.renttherunway.com

Clothes swaps

How about doing clothes swaps with your friends and siblings? It's a fun way to wear something new to you!

Alternatively, you can attend or even set up a clothes swap at your school or in your community! Read this great article by Karina Schönberger

https://www.sustainyourstyle.org/en/blog/2020/6/25/how-to-organize-a-clothes-swap

For sharing clothes, try the link below, or speak with your friends and set up your own little group.

https://www.thenuwardrobe.com

What to do when clothes get damaged

When your clothes get damaged, such as holes, mend them to extend their 'life'. You can buy cheap sewing kits from many different places and there are hundreds of YouTube tutorials on mending clothes. If you are absolutely incapable of sewing, you can find places on Yelp where people can mend your clothes for you. But it is cheaper to mend clothes yourself and you can add your personal touches that make them individual to you.

What to do with clothes that are beyond repair or are too small

There are hundreds of DIYs you can do for irreparable pieces of clothing. You can make tote bags from t-shirts, cloths from rags, there are so many different things you can do, so get creative!

When your clothes are too small, there are a few more options available. One option is giving it to somebody you know, like a younger sibling or friend. As an idea, you can organise clothes swaps with your friends! (see earlier notes)

Another option is to sell it. This could be on eBay, DEPOP or other similar apps and websites.

This last option should only be a last resort. The last option is to donate. I say this should be a last resort because there is no guarantee that the clothes will actually be donated. A large proportion of donated clothes end up in landfills, so it is best to try the previous options instead.

Washing and drying your clothes

Washing and drying your clothes have a bigger environmental impact than you may think. Fortunately, all of these negative environmental impacts can be solved easily *sigh of relief*. One thing to do is pretty basic, and that is to only wash full machines, as this is more efficient than washing say five small loads. One more basic thing is to wear your clothes more than once before putting it in the wash as this will reduce the amount that needs to be washed in a week, which will save energy.

You can also wash on low temperatures, or better still, use eco-programming if that's an option on your washing machine. This will save energy since heating the water in a washing machine consumes the most amount of energy.

Also, you could use a washing bag. This prevents microplastics from being released into the ocean.

The last thing you can do in relation to washing is use environmentally friendly detergents and softeners.

For drying, air dry as much as you can! This saves a lot of energy and it makes your fabrics last longer. You also don't have to worry about your clothes shrinking.

What you can do this week

- Search some news stories on a few clothing brands. Do they have a history of poor treatment towards their workers?

- Go into your wardrobe and look at the materials of your clothes (does it say where it was made?).

- Look at the environmental and social efforts made by some popular brands (if there are any).

- Take the ThredUp clothes footprint quiz. Are you surprised with your results? https://www.thredup.com/fashionfootprint

- If you want to, go to your wardrobe or wherever you keep your clothes and have a clear out. Decide which clothes you actually like and get rid of the ones you rarely wear. Sell the clothes you no longer want or give them to a friend or neighbour.

- If you want to, buy some clothes from DEPOP, ThredUp or ethical clothing brands.

Well done for completing this week's chapter!

End of chapter checklist ✔

1. Avoid buying clothes that are made with environmentally damaging materials if you can.

2. Avoid purchasing clothes from brands that have poor working conditions for their staff, including sweatshops.

3. Buy less clothes.

4. Buy clothes from more sustainable brands if possible.

5. Buy or inherit clothes second hand (this reduces your carbon footprint by 60-70%).

6. Mend clothes instead of throwing them away.

7. Make some DIYs with old/worn out clothes.

8. Wear clothes more than once before putting them in the wash.

9. Wash clothes on low temperatures.

10. Air-dry clothes more often.

11. Use environmentally-friendly detergents and softeners.

12. Use a washing bag.

13. Download 'Shoptagr' (a browser extension that alerts you on offers and sales on items of clothing - this can come in handy for the more expensive pieces).

Statistics in the 'End of chapter checklist' are from ThredUp

Advocating for the planet

Now that you know what you can do to reduce your impact on the environment, it's time to advocate for the planet.

Advocating is what I think to be the most important topic in this book. This is because advocation helps to make people live more environmentally friendly lifestyles on a larger scale. It's great if you follow the tips that I have given in this book, but only governments can implement the long-term and wide-spread changes that we need for a sustainable future.

Protesting and activism

We have definitely seen positive change as a result of protesting. By protesting, Greta Thunberg has undeniably brought more awareness to climate change.

To go to a school-strike is a decision you should make with your parent/guardian or your school, as you need their permission to miss school. By asking for permission, you can strike legally. If you do attend a protest, be safe. Look at legal advice before attending a protest. The UKSCN (UK Student Climate Network) has a page on their website that informs you on legal advice for UK students.

https://ukscn.org/legal-advice/

If you cannot attend a protest, just remember that it doesn't make you any less of a climate activist than those who do attend! There are still other ways you can be an activist. Other ways include through photography, drawing, song-writing, journalism, and more. There are so many different ways to be an activist!

Petitions

Petitions, whether you create one or you sign one, can make a positive change. One successful petition all started with two girls called Ella and Caitlin. Their petition on Change.org resulted in Burger King® and McDonalds® no longer giving out hard plastic toys in the UK. This is fantastic news! When everyone comes together, organisations and brands will listen, and change their environmentally damaging ways.

School and the environment

You can help raise awareness about environmental issues at school! You can do this by starting an environment club where you can discuss the problems that threaten the planet and what you can do to reduce your school's impact. Some things you can do include:

- Eliminating single-use plastic from the cafeteria like cutlery

- Introduce a better recycling scheme

- Encourage people to switch off the lights when they leave the room (or have the school invest in automatic lights which would save money on electricity bills too)

and more......

Re-Earth Initiative https://fliphtml5.com/bookcase/jaxfx has lots of tips on what you can do to reduce your school's impact in their toolkits! They also have other tips for reducing your community's environmental impact as well.

Writing a letter or email to your constituency's representative

It's your representative's job to raise constituents' concerns to the government. How are they supposed to raise your concerns about the environment if you don't write to them? By writing to your representative, you can make a difference. This may seem a bit daunting for you and you may be unsure on how to write to your representative but lucky for you, I have some tips!

How to write a letter or email to your representative

- Find out who your local representative is. You can search up 'Who is my local MP/MOC/ (or whatever a political representative is called in your country)'.

- Look at their stance on the environment and climate change.

- Search your representative's contact details.

- Before writing your letter or email, think about your concerns when it comes to the environment. Which issues do you want to focus on? This can be plastic pollution, fossil fuels, environmental laws and policies, etcetera.

- Write the letter or email

How to structure a letter or email to your representative

- Always address your representative formally by using their correct title(s).

- Inform them that you are a constituent of their constituency.

- Tell them why you are writing to them (which environmental issue are you going to be voicing concern for?).

- Tell them why you are concerned and why they should be too. Use solid evidence and statistics to express your concern.

- Write about the solutions that are available for this environmental issue. Also write about how it is cost-effective, and why it is important that this issue is solved.

- Tell them what they should do next.

- Sign off your letter or email correctly.

In your letter or email, be formal throughout and avoid the use of contractions, e.g. I am instead of I'm.

You should also keep your letter or email concise but informative and don't stray from the topic. Another tip is to mention the environmental policies already in place for this specific issue (if there are any), and to use lots of key terminology such as green gentrification[1]. This will make them respect you more as it will be clear that you have lots of knowledge in this area.

Green gentrification[1]- is a process of cleaning up pollution or planting lots of green plants in a neighbourhood that once was polluted to increase property value and attract wealthy people. This is bad as it displaces and excludes poorer residents.

Postscripts note: *We can all make changes to how we live, but the REAL change comes from governments and politicians. They can create and enforce policies and laws that protect and preserve our environment, how we farm it, use and manage its natural resources, manufacturing processes, packaging standards and how we deal with waste.*

Having a conversation with somebody about the climate crisis

Having a conversation about the climate crisis to people who don't care about the environment can be difficult, especially if they're not open to changing their views and lifestyle. Below I've got some tips on how to have a conversation with somebody about the climate crisis.

1. Understand your own values: before having a conversation, understand your own values. Why is the environment important to you? Is it because other people are suffering because of climate change? Is it because of the animals? Take a look at yourself and find out which environmental causes are most important to you.

2. Understand their values: before having a conversation, understand what their values are. Think about the experiences they have had which may have made them think this way? What are they passionate about? It's important to know how the other person thinks as this will allow you to have a more meaningful and personal discussion. This will make the person more engaged in the discussion.

3. Casually bring it up: suddenly bringing up the topic could make people feel that you have caught them off-guard and make them unwilling to have a conversation. You could bring it up by saying 'Hey, have you seen the news recently?' (Talk about an environmental issue that has happened recently, because unfortunately they happen all the time, so there is bound to be one on the news).

4. Ask them what they think: ask them what they think and how they feel about that news story? Does it make them feel upset? Do they not care?

5. Ask them why they think or feel that way: understand why and you will be able to create solutions.

6. Listen: listen to what they have to say, even if it may frustrate you at times, it is important to stay calm and collected. Getting angry will just make things escalate and upset the other person. Listening will also help you to understand where the other person if coming from. It's important to respect other people's opinions, even if you don't agree with them.

7. Challenge their views: challenge their views in a polite and constructive way. If you know any statistics or evidence, talk about it.

8. Be patient: it's unlikely that someone will change their views after one conversation - it takes time. Continue to have conversations with people about climate change.

Documentaries and films: watch documentaries and films about environmental issues. This could help them see the undeniable evidence supporting ideas of climate change and environmental issues.

Some fantastic documentaries include:

• 'War on Plastic' - available on BBC iPlayer.

• 'Before the Flood' - available on Disney+.

• 'The True Cost' - available on Amazon and True Cost website.

Talk to them about solutions: once they have realised the damage that has been done to the planet, talk to them about what they can do.

Sorry if I sounded like a WikiHow article in this section

How to Fix the Planet (When you're a Teenager)

What you can do this week

- Sign some petitions!

- Write a letter or email to your MP.

- Write a letter or email to a brand.

- Talk to someone about the climate crisis.

Well done for completing this week's chapter!

End of chapter checklist ✔

1. Sign important environmental petitions.

2. Help your school become more environmentally-friendly (create a club!).

3. Write a letter to your MP.

4. Protest for climate justice.

5. Have conversations with people about the climate crisis.

6. Spread awareness about the climate crisis and what people can do to help!

Well done! ☺

I f you're reading this, you've probably just finished the book (or just skipped to the end…maybe that's just me, I'm impatient, I can't help it!). For those who have finished the book and have started to make lifestyle changes, I just want to say well done. Well done for reading this book, well done for practising my tips in your life, well done for being you. I know that the last bit was quite corny, but I mean it.

We need people like you to change the world!

So, carry on recycling, reducing, refusing, reusing, repairing, protesting, changing, advocating and Thank you for doing your bit!

My generation may be the last letter of the alphabet, but we are also the begining of the next way of living, for we of the present are ALL accountable for the future. **Together, we can fix the planet.**

cue weirdly uplifting music that comes at the end of a 2000s movie

~~Gossip Girl~~ Jen Zead

xoxo

If you want to know more about what I am up to day to day, follow Jen Zead on instagram and twitter

Further reading

Interested in UK government Strategic Communications: Behaviour Approach? Go here https://gcs.civilservice.gov.uk/publications/strategic-communications-a-behavioural-approach/

Interested in Tropical rain forests as carbon sinks by E. Soepadmo in Chemosphere? Go here https://www.sciencedirect.com/science/article/abs/pii/004565359390066E

Interested in Bridging the gap - the role of low carbon lifestyles by Adam Corner from Climate Outreach? Go here https://climateoutreach.org/bridging-gap-role-of-low-carbon-lifestyles

Interested in The Plastics Paradox by UKRI scientists including Professor Miodownik? Go here https://www.ukri.org/our-work/delivering-economic-impact/the-plastics-paradox/

Interested in Can we feed future population of 10 billion on a healthy diet… by the EAT-Lancet Commission on Food, Planet, Health? I think you get the gist, go here https://eatforum.org/eat-lancet-commission/

Interested in Microplastics ? Go here https://www.nationalgeographic.co.uk/environment/2019/06/you-eat-thousands-bits-plastic-every-year

Interested in Fast Fashion? Go here https://www.greenpeace.org.uk/news/fast-fashion-this-industry-needs-an-urgent-makeover/?source=GA&subsource=GOFRNAOAGA034J&gclid=EAIaIQobChMIwqr5qZvs7gIVBtN3Ch2p4gC_EAAYASAAEgI3-fD_BwE

Interested in new Material routes, a Burberry scoping report? Go here https://rca-media2.rca.ac.uk/documents/BMFRG_Catalogue_Scoping_Project_LDF18.pdf

Acknowledgements

I would like to thank the following people for their valuable time and enthusiasm to help me reach the point of publishing this book:

Heather MacRae (Chief Executive Ideas Foundation), for her ideas and encouragement (you started all of this ☺).

Ted Smith (Chair of Ideas Foundation) for initial words of encouragement and advice.

Professor Mark Miodownik from UCL for your invaluable comments on plastics.

Bruna Petreca from Royal College of Art for your deep insights and understanding regarding fabrics.

Prof Effie Papargyropoulou at Leeds University for inspiration and motivation.

Sam Angel from TerraCycle for detailed insights and advice.

Mathilde Charpall (founder of Sustain Your Style) for diligently reviewing the chapter on clothing.

Kieran Kiggell from UKSCN for his thorough review of the chapter on advocating.

Dr Jennifer Lucey from the University of Oxford for her great insights into Palm Oil (I have learnt so much!)

Clare Dudeney from Sustainability First for inspiration and encouragement.

Adam Corner & Roz Pidcock from Climate Outreach for support and advice.

Acknowledgements contd.

Rhianna Hillier for her diligent proofreading.

Miss Patel, her ongoing encouragement and enthusiasm for this book.

All of you, thank you for your time, the review of the various chapters and wonderful comments. I have learnt much from each of you.

A massive thanks to Hannah Lacey from UKRI NERC for giving up her free time to help me find the right people to provide comments and fact check the book. Kudos, Hannah!

An 'out of this world' (sorry, I couldn't help myself) THANK YOU to Richard Garriott – extraordinary explorer – for taking such an interest in this book, providing review comments, encouragement, and willingness to write the foreword!

I am truly humbled to have met, virtually, all of the above people who have willingly given up their spare time to review my book, provide their comments and support! You are all amazing and inspirational!

A special thanks to my parents and sister for letting this book take over our lives for a while until I got it published. Thank you for not letting me give up!

9 781838 417802